Jesus – more than a prophet

JESUS
more than a prophet

Edited by R W F Wootton

Inter-Varsity Press
STL Books, Bromley

Inter-Varsity Press
38 De Montfort Street, Leicester LE1 7GP, England

First published 1982
Reprinted 1984, 1986

British Library Cataloguing in Publication Data
Wootton, Richard W. F.
    Jesus – more than a prophet
    1. Converts from Islam
    I. Title
    248.2′46   BV 2625
    ISBN 0-85110-422-3 (IVP)
    ISBN 0-903843-81-1 (STL)

Set in Baskerville
Typeset in Great Britain by TJB Photosetting
Printed in Great Britain by Collins, Glasgow

*Inter-Varsity Press is the publishing division of the Universities and
Colleges Christian Fellowship (formerly the Inter-Varsity Fellowship),
a student movement linking Christian Unions in universities and
colleges throughout the United Kingdom and the Republic of Ireland,
and a member movement of the International Fellowship of Evangelical
Students.
For information about local and national activities write to
UCCF, 38 De Montfort Street, Leicester LE1 7GP.*

*STL Books are published by Send The Light (Operation Mobilisation),
PO Box 48, Bromley, Kent, England*

Contents

Preface   6

1   The old Ghulam is dead   9

2   The dynamic of love   14

3   I had found the fountain of life   18

4   Everyone will pay homage to Jesus   23

5   I was forgiven   26

6   The joy that I have found   30

7   Everything became different   34

8   How can I be reconciled to a holy God?   38

9   Pastor of all the town   42

10   The giver of salvation and peace   47

11   I will serve him all my life   52

12   The pearl of great price   58

13   A total self-awakening   63

14   Christ helps me to live life to the full   69

15   It was all that I had longed for   73

A brief statement of the Christian faith   77

5

Preface

The history of the relations of Christians and Muslims
down the centuries is on the whole a sad and shameful one.
Christians have not lived up to their duty to love their
neighbours (of whatever creed) as themselves; nor have
Muslims always taken seriously the Prophet's word, 'Thou
wilt find the nearest of them in affection to those who
believe to be those who say, Lo, we are Christians' (Quran
5:82). Whatever Christians have suffered at various times
from Muslims, they may safely acknowledge the shameful
crimes committed by their forefathers against the people of
Islam, especially during the Crusades and the period of
colonial exploitation, now happily ended.

The bitter and long-continued struggle in the past leaves
its legacy today. This is especially sad when we see how
much is held in common: belief in one true and living
God, the maker of heaven and earth, of angels and men,
who has spoken through the prophets (of whom a long line
is recognized in common by both faiths), who has revealed
his holy will to men and demands worship and obedience
from them, who hears their prayers and one day will call
them to judgment, who alone is to be glorified, exalted and
adored, God blessed for ever! Amen.

It is true that the differences between the two faiths are
substantial and touch on the very nature of God. But it is
good indeed that in recent years Christians and Muslims
have begun to sit down together. They have learnt to speak

and listen to each other, to remove misunderstandings (which are common on both sides). They have examined what is held jointly by both faiths without ignoring the differences, and explored the riches of the other faith. Real benefit has already come from this process of 'dialogue'. But this does not mean the suspension of mission or *da'wah* (invitation) by either side. Christians recognize the right of Muslims in Britain and elsewhere to propagate their faith and to make converts from people of other faiths or no faith; and this they are doing, not without success. But Christians also claim the right to bear witness to what they believe to be the truth before the people of Islam, in obedience to the commands of the Lord Jesus, who told his followers to make disciples from all nations.

This collection of brief life-stories is a part of that witness. It is not a study book for those who want to learn all the basic teachings of Islam, though the stories highlight key areas of belief and practice. Instead we hope that Christians will read the book to gain insight into the faith and life of their Muslim friends, and that Muslims will read it to find out the things which led their former co-religionists to profess the Christian faith. There is no suggestion, of course, that any of the stories, particularly their details, should be seen as the 'standard' experience of those coming to faith in Christ. The sovereign Lord deals differently with each of us.

The stories are written by all kinds of people in many different lands and, with two exceptions, in their own words. Some are wealthy and highly educated, and some are from humble backgrounds. At no point do the writers deny the good in Islam, indeed many retain a deep respect for it. Their experience centres on Jesus (*'Isa*), the one whom the Quran and Muslim orthodoxy accept as born by a virgin, as the worker of many miracles, as living a sinless life, as taken up alive into heaven and destined to return to the earth at the end of the world. They are simply concerned to tell how God has become real to them in a completely new way through Jesus, their Saviour and Lord, and how

7

they have found a new meaning to life and the assurance of salvation in the world to come through him. We hope their words may be read with an open mind and a willingness to seek the truth wherever it may be found.

1
The old Ghulam is dead

How can God forgive me when I have killed so many innocent people? I wanted to pray, but my heart was gripped with sudden fear. What would it be like to fall into the hands of an angry God?

G M NAAMAN of Pakistan was drawn into the bitter conflict which attended the partition of India in 1947, and fought hard for Islam. The inhumanity of that time left him troubled in spirit, with an unsatisfied longing for God. Then Christ found him and made him a new person, putting peace in his heart despite opposition. His new life of service for Christ continues today in the ministry of the Church of Pakistan.

I was born in 1930 in the city of Jammu in North India, the youngest of five brothers in a Muslim family of good standing. My father was a Subedar-Major in the Indian Army, observing the laws of Islam, but with a difference – he had a feeling for mysticism, for an inner knowledge of God; he was in fact a Sufi.

When I was five, we moved to the old town of Zaffarwal, in the Punjab but close to the border of Jammu and Kashmir. The headmaster of my school was also a Sufi, and some of my class-fellows were Christians. There was a Christian congregation in the town with the Rev. Ibrahim, a former Muslim, as its pastor. As a child I was impressed by the devotion of a woman evangelist, who was always talking to people of Jesus and his love. I could see that her faith meant everything to her. At the age of nine I went back to Jammu to high school, where a very different atmosphere prevailed, for most of the teachers were Hindus. I did quite well at school, but by the age of thirteen I was bored with it and ran away to join the Indian Air Force, serving on the Burma Front.

The days after the war were very difficult for me. As a boy I had sympathized with the movement for national independence, and I was suspected of belonging to a seditious organization. My position in the Air Force became difficult and I was released in May 1947. I returned to my mother and brothers at Jammu; my father had recently died. Here I found a sad change. The whole country was in a ferment, with the prospect of independence near at last, but a bitter conflict was raging between Muslims on one side and Hindus and Sikhs on the other.

As feelings rose to fever pitch, a *jihad* or holy war for Islam was proclaimed in the mosques of the Punjab, and I too was swept into the struggle to fight for my Muslim brethren in Jammu, as a member of the 'Azad (Free) Kashmir' forces. I proved a keen and efficient soldier, and recall with shame how I joined others in setting fire to villages, sometimes putting unarmed people to death and sometimes forcing them to embrace Islam. At times my conscience would be shocked, as on the occasion when I came across a Hindu girl being forced to gratify the soldiers' desires. I grew more and more depressed, for I had been brought up in a good world where simple people loved one another and where I had all I could want.

In one village I found two middle-aged Christian men and said to them, 'Why don't you become Muslims?' They did not answer, but a girl of twelve with them called out, 'We cannot!' I said, 'Then you'll have to face the consequences!' 'Yes,' she replied, 'but the one in whom we believe has said, "Lo, I am with you always, to the close of the age".' Then the three of them knelt down and prayed, calling on Jesus Christ. When they got up, I said, 'Forgive me for what I have done', and the answer came, 'We forgive you in Jesus' name.' I felt compelled not only to spare them but also to give them some of the things which we had taken from others.

On another occasion we had set fire to a village and were waiting to shoot the people who ran out. Suddenly an old woman ran towards us carrying a little child, whom she dropped at my feet, crying, 'Kill him! Your religion is to kill people and your God can only be pleased when you kill others. But remember this – God can never be pleased when you kill his handiwork.'

I looked down at the child, sobbing frightened at my feet; I felt stunned and for some minutes could not speak. A wave of loathing for what I was doing swept over me. I said softly to the woman, 'Take the child, and before God I tell you these hands of mine will never again kill anyone for the sake of religion.' At last I knew how great a sinner I was, and I asked myself, 'How can God forgive me when I have killed so many innocent people?' A terror of black darkness came over me. My thoughts of Islamic belief and practice gradually faded from my mind and I found myself an agnostic. I sent in my resignation from the 'Azad Kashmir' forces and was allowed to leave on condition that I slipped away quietly without telling anyone why.

But where to go and what to do? I wanted to pray, but my heart was gripped with sudden fear. What would it be like to fall into the hands of an angry God?' I found no help from friends or brothers when I told them I had lost faith in Islam. With a troubled spirit I decided to leave my brothers and mother.

One night I came to Kamaliya railway station, my heart filled with a deep but unsatisfied longing for God. In the waiting-room at midnight I opened my heart to him, praying, 'O God, help me – I want to meet you!' As I prayed, I seemed to hear a voice saying, 'My grace is sufficient for you', and at this word all my burden of sorrow and depression rolled away. As I repeated the words many times a Christian cleaner came in and heard me – he recognized the words and told me they were St Paul's (2 Corinthians 12:9).

Not far away was a Christian village, and there I went to visit the pastor, telling him that I wished to become a Christian. He sent me off with a note to the town of Gojra, twenty-five miles away, where there was an important Anglican Church centre, with an Englishman in charge.

There, on a hot afternoon, he listened to me attentively as I told him some of my experiences and my spiritual quest. To engage his interest and sympathy, I told him that I had a wife who had died suddenly. This was not true. He welcomed me warmly, saying that I should stay there for some weeks, so that I could be quite sure about my decision to be baptized and they could be satisfied of my genuineness.

I was given a little room and a bed, and I began to study the Christian faith systematically. I found a friend and helper in a nightwatchman, Buta Masih, a man of simple and living faith. We prayed and read the New Testament together daily. One night when the Englishman was sitting on his bed before going to sleep, I reminded him of what I had told him about my wife's death, then blurted out, 'Well, that wasn't true, and now that I've come to know the Lord I can't continue in a lie.' He was moved by this confession, and together we thanked God for working in this way in my heart.

I attended the first Gojra Christian Convention and found the talks very helpful, but the greatest moment for me was on the Sunday when I stood up before a large congregation, acknowledged my faith in Jesus Christ and was baptized. Till then I had been Ghulam Rasul, Servant of the Apostle (Muhammad); now I became Ghulam Masih, Servant of Christ.

Soon after this my brothers came to fetch me, saying my mother was ill. I found her well, but very upset at my having become a Christian. My brothers called in some Islamic teachers to argue with me; but they could make no impression and left me with angry words and threats.

Then my brothers beat me severely and shut me up in a room for days without food. But my faith sustained me, and they could only wonder at my patience under suffering. When they expressed their surprise that I seemed so different from before, I told them, 'I am a new man; the old Ghulam is dead now. I have a new way of behaviour and a new attitude to life.' I felt my life was in danger, but I remembered the words of that great Punjabi Christian, Sundar Singh, 'It is easy to die for Christ, but hard to live for him; dying takes an hour or two, but to live for him means to die daily.'

Soon I felt God's call to go out and preach, so I became a roving evangelist, visiting Christians of all denominations and speaking wherever ministers gave me permission. In Zaffarwal I proclaimed my faith in a procession of witness before those who had known me as a boy. Then I went to Sind and learned Sindhi, taking part in the annual 'eye camp' at Shikarpur, where thousands of patients and their relatives came each year for eye treatment from Christian doctors. In 1952 I was asked to work among the Kohli people in Sind, Hindus who at first would not accept me, so that I had to camp outside a village under a tree. But God used me to heal some by laying on hands with prayer and I received a warm welcome.

Soon after that I was sent to the Gujranwala Theological Seminary to train for the Christian ministry. Later I spoke twice in Karachi to a group of nurses in the vacation. One was a young Punjabi called Daisy; she came from a Christian home but was proud and self-satisfied. God used my words to pierce the armour of her pride, so that she repented with tears and yielded to Christ. This drew us together, and I was very happy when her parents were willing to arrange our marriage. She has been a wonderful strength and help to me ever since. Just after our marriage I took the name Naaman, after the Syrian general who found healing for leprosy at the hands of the prophet Elisha because of the witness of a young servant girl – the witness of Christian women has meant so much to me.

2
The dynamic of love

The very tradition and culture that gave meaning and depth to my life stirred profound questions in my mind: questions about God and man, about life and death and ultimate reality. These sent me back to the Quran, and there one thing appealed to me: its testimony to Jesus Christ, prophet and apostle, but not the crucified.

LAMIN OUSMAN SANNEH comes from the Mandinka people of Gambia. At first deeply committed to Islam, he pondered deeply on ultimate questions. The Quran turned his thoughts to Jesus. Reading the Bible, he came to realize that God loved him just as he was, and this changed his whole life. Since his conversion he has served with 'Islam in Africa', has taken a London Ph.D. in Islamic studies, and is now on the staff of Aberdeen University.

In my boyhood days when the fast of Ramadan was approaching there was a tremendous atmosphere of excitement among us, a feeling of community solidarity, of belonging together. I looked forward to it with great enthusiasm, and I always welcomed this time appointed for men to adore God, to submit to God, the focus of our religious devotion. Sometimes I wanted to escape from its rigorous observance; there was a feeling that God is stern and inflexible in his demands. But along with this there

14

was a great sense of accomplishing the one thing that God had laid down. Of course the feast day that followed the fast was a glorious day. I enjoyed the food and going to the prayer ground with all my friends in my clean robes; there was a glorious feeling of being accepted before God because of fulfilling my obligations to him.

I went to an all-Muslim boarding school, where on special days we would pray the whole night and, as the dawn was breaking, our hymns of praise ascended to God – it seemed that with the daybreak God's mercy was breaking upon us. This is the sort of religious discipline I had as a Muslim, and I am very grateful for it.

You may wonder why in spite of all this I became a Christian. The very tradition and culture that gave meaning and depth to my life stirred profound questions in my mind: questions about God and man, about life and death and ultimate reality. These sent me back to the Quran, and there one thing appealed to me: its testimony to Jesus Christ, prophet and apostle, but not the crucified, for in the Quran 'somebody else' was put in his place. I was interested in death and the life after death, and it struck me that if God was personally involved in taking someone else and exchanging him for Jesus on the cross, then God bore responsibility for whoever died there.

Then I thought, 'Supposing Jesus did die on the cross, and God intended it so?' I reflected on the suffering and the heart-break and the hopes dashed to pieces which are a part of life, and it seemed to me that deep down at the centre and core of life the cross was declaring something about the inner mystery of life. And so I became very interested in the life of Christ. Then I came to accept as a historical event that Jesus Christ died on the cross, and ultimately reached the conclusion that he died for me, for my sins.

My acceptance of Christ came from the Quran. After it I was led into reading the Bible and came upon the fantastic declaration that God loves me just as I am and is not interested in whether I have good points to add up. One of

15

the greatest stumbling-blocks to a realization that God loves us as we are, is our trying to be good, to impress God with our acts of service and kindness. Or sometimes we go to the other extreme, we become despondent about our sins, we confess them to God and play on his pity. But the wonderful thing is that according to the New Testament God loves me just as I am – this made a tremendous difference in my life.

When I tried to join the church I met with difficulties. They were not used to people like me and were reluctant to accept me. I had to fight my way and insist that I belonged. Someone said to me, 'You must be very important for God to have called you from Islam', and this tempted me to pride. It was easy to underrate the church and say, 'They're all bad; I don't want to belong with them.' And when Muslim friends stoned me in the street and abused me I was tempted to turn round and call down God's wrath on them.

In these situations God showed me that the cross of Calvary is a constant, unchangeable fact which transforms your life all the time, whatever situation you are in. Whatever our feelings may be, God loves us – because the cross is there, and what a relief that is! This is partly the secret of the Psalmist's words, 'Whither shall I flee from thy presence?' God's presence is his love which is always there, surrounding and embracing us. The apostle John said, 'See what love the Father has given us.' God loves me just as I am.

The apostle Paul speaks of us as pots of earthenware containing a treasure, and this treasure is God himself. If we know this, then we want to make it known to everyone, and that is why we go to the Muslim.

After further study of Islam and Arabic in England and the Lebanon, I went back to Africa seeking to help the churches to get close to Muslim people. When we really come to know that God loves us, it means that he has faith in us, so much that he has entrusted himself in Christ Jesus into our hands. The only way we can make him known is by the dynamic of love.

I praise God for the way he raised me up, and for everything he has given me. I praise him too for all the tremendous gifts and treasures bestowed on me in the discipline of my Muslim upbringing. These he wants me to use to his glory, to declare that the inner secret of all my upbringing is Christ Jesus, enthroned on the right hand of God, and to declare this in love, in humility, in patience and service and in thanksgiving – in everything giving thanks to the Lord.

3
I had found
the fountain of life

I was puzzled as to why Muslims were afraid of reading the Bible. I therefore decided to read it more seriously and whole-heartedly, and prayed to Almighty God to guide me . . . . As I read it . . . my objections to the Christian faith evaporated.

As a young man ASLAM KHAN was a deeply earnest Muslim. He became involved in religious controversy, which led him to study the Bible in order to refute it. Instead his eyes were opened to God's offer of free forgiveness in Christ; a salvation which no-one can earn. Life began again for him, and since then he has proclaimed the good news about Jesus, often at the risk of his own life. For many years he has served as a much-respected evangelist and minister in the church in Pakistan.

I come from a respectable Muslim family of Gujrat in Pakistan. My father owned land and our family was one of the most influential in the area. I was the only son and my father showered all the best things of this life on me. He gave me the best education according to his standards, and appointed a very learned 'maulvi' to instruct me in Islam and other allied subjects. As my father was an orthodox Muslim, he wanted me to understand the beauties of his religion and to propagate its tenets to others.

When I completed my primary education at the village school, my father accepted a government post in Rajasthan (north west India). I was admitted to a Christian high school where Bible lessons were given to both Christians and non-Christians alike. This conflicted with my training, and so I made it a point not to attend the Bible classes, in spite of great pressure from the headmaster. In addition, I was so proud of my family name that I did not like to mix with Christian students at the school, who were the children of poor families. I had no interest in Christians and felt no attraction for their religion. I used to think that the British people were trying to bribe the poverty-stricken people of this country to embrace their way of life and religion.

At this period it so happened that a man recently converted from Islam visited Rajasthan, and he came to our town as well. The local Christians arranged a few meetings to enable him to give his testimony. I attended some of these meetings with my father, who put several difficult questions to the learned speaker, and I had the impression that he failed to answer them adequately. This deepened my hatred of Christians and their religion, and I also picked up the habit of teasing and harassing Christian padres and evangelists wherever I came across them. It was my firm belief that my religion – Islam – was the only true religion, and that it was the highest form of religion in the world.

In those days some members of the Arya Samaj sect, a defensive movement among Hindus, were re-converting Malkanas, a community of Hindus who had become Muslims. Their movement is called 'shuddhi', which means purification by reclamation to the old Hindu faith. It was a matter of great importance to me to check this movement, and so I immediately decided to offer my services for a counter-movement against the Arya Samaj. My opponents therefore found a great enemy in me, so they began to harm me in every possible way. One day while I was sleeping in a hut they came stealthily and broke down the roof. This caused me severe injuries, and I had to stay in bed for several days. This intensified my hatred for other

19

religions, and I used all my strength against the Arya Samaj.

All these incidents made me an advocate and a speaker for my Muslim co-religionists. My fame spread far and wide and I got an opportunity to attend a conference of religions at Mainpuri (U.P., India). This conference was arranged by the Arya Samaj, and they had invited leaders from all religions. It proved very fruitful for me, as it stimulated me to study other faiths. I immediately purchased their literature and started to study it, mainly to find fault and to show the superiority of my ancestral religion. Hindu literature did not satisfy my spiritual hunger, but I began to take some interest in the Holy Bible.

One day my father saw me studying the Scriptures and this upset him very much. He ordered me to stop doing so, thus betraying his fear that by reading it I might change my religion and become a Christian. I did not believe this, but I was puzzled as to why Muslims were afraid of reading the Bible. I therefore decided to read it more seriously and whole-heartedly, and prayed to Almighty God to guide me. As I read it with the heart of a child it began to influence my soul, and by the operation of the Holy Spirit my objections to the Christian faith evaporated.

As I studied the Bible the hidden mysteries of the faith were revealed to me, and so my own findings proved to be quite different from the ideas which my father entertained about Christianity. I found the Bible the only book of salvation, the only record of God's revelation of love for mankind. To me the Bible proved to be a hidden treasure that saves man from the curse of sin and gives him eternal life through Jesus Christ. 'If any one is in Christ, he is a new creation; the old has passed away, behold, the new has come' (2 Corinthians 5:17).

Now I realized that salvation is a gift of God. The injunction to earn it by good deeds is an impossible enterprise. Paul's words are a great guide against such a misconception: 'For I know that nothing good dwells within me ... For I do not do the good I want, but the evil that I do not want is what I do ... Wretched man that I am! Who will deliver me from this body of death?' (Romans 7:18, 19, 24) and 'All have sinned and fall short of the glory of God' (Romans 3:23).

My conclusion was that no human being can attain salvation through his own efforts. Even the Quran taught me that the entire human race is sinful and that the only innocent and pure person is the Lord Jesus Christ. Our Lord challenged the critics of his own time, 'Which of you convicts me of sin?' (John 8:46). So I was convinced that Christ alone is pure, and his purity is the purity of God.

After the disclosure of this secret there was nothing now for me to find in the Quran. I had found the fountain of divine Life which washes away the dirt of the sinner and gives him eternal life. This experience made me both sad and happy. I was sad to think that I must sever my connection with my ancestral faith in which I was deeply rooted. I was happy because I had found my Saviour, the Lord Jesus. I therefore spent most of my time in prayer and study of the Bible for further guidance.

One day as I opened my Bible my eyes fell on the comforting words of our Lord in Matthew 11:28: 'Come to me, all who labour and are heavy laden, and I will give you rest.' The Lord himself gave me a message of comfort and peace. Later I went to a Christian minister and asked him to baptize me. He questioned me thoroughly on various points, and after due preparation baptized me on October 27th 1928.

After that a new chapter in my life opened. All my relations deserted me and I became a homeless wanderer. My wife did not join me at that time, but I prayed for her and she also decided to become a Christian. After her conversion we both worked together for the Lord, to spread the good news. We have served in a number of places in Pakistan. For some years I have been the evangelist at St Andrew's Brotherhood, Lahore. This is a voluntary society supported by Pakistani Christians, without any regular financial help from any of the churches. I run the centre for enquirers and converts, to which many have come during our time there. Thus we share with others the wonderful message of God's love for us in Christ, which has come to mean so much to us.

4
Everyone will pay homage to Jesus

I began to study the gospel carefully. There was a power in it which said to me, 'You, Jahangir, are a sinner and an enemy of God. There is no true peace through good works.' This was true for me, for though a much-respected and wealthy family man I had no peace of heart. I was full of pride.

MR JAHANGIR was a proud member of a noble and strictly Muslim family of Pathans. A New Testament given by a missionary convinced him that before God he was a sinner needing salvation. He put his faith in Christ, and when he was baptized he had a marvellous experience of the reality and the nearness of his Lord and Saviour. Since then Jahangir has borne witness to him among the Muslim people of Sind.

My name is Jahangir, son of Khair Ullah Khan, and I am connected with the Durranis, the former royal house of Afghanistan. My family moved about a hundred years ago to Sind and became wealthy land-owners in the ancient city of Shikarpur. Being a Pathan I am well acquainted with Islam, for Pathans are very strict Muslims and observers of the Islamic law. My parents were strict and temperate people, and they introduced me and my brothers thoroughly to the secrets of Islam. Today my elder brother is a champion of the Shiah faith and I am a soldier of Christ.

Several years ago when I was running a furniture shop a missionary evangelist came to the shop with some chairs. In the course of conversation he spoke to me about the Bible and about Christ. I did not take much notice, for my mind was steeped in the law, and it was impossible for me to recognize God's grace so quickly. Later I went to his house and he gave me a book called 'The Holy Gospel'. I began to study it carefully. There was a power in it which said to me, 'You, Jahangir, are a sinner and an enemy of God. There is no true peace through good works.' This was true for me, for though a much-respected and wealthy family man I had no peace of heart. I was full of pride. I remember still the verse which speaks of the gospel as power – 'the power of God for salvation to every one who has faith' (Romans 1:16).

I grew more and more troubled. I believed in God as judge, and I read that salvation is through Christ (Acts 4:12) and judgment has been ended in Christ through his cross. But it was impossible for me to abandon Islam and believe in Christ. Yet daily I read the New Testament attentively. My character was changing; people were astonished to see that the man who used to be so proud had become so meek.

In this troubled state I gave myself to prayer. One night, which was for me the first and last of my life, I heard a voice say, 'The cure of a troubled spirit is faith, the faith that Jesus is the Messiah and the Son of God. If you want to join God's family, then call his Son Lord.' I did not know who was speaking thus to me. In the morning I made a firm intention of believing in Christ. Then to make the matter clearer and my resolve stronger I read the Muslim tradition which says that on the last day everyone will pay homage to Jesus. I said to myself, 'Then it will be compulsory – I will do it now.'

People got to know that Durrani was reading the gospel. Many came and told me not to read it, saying, 'It's changed; you'll be misled; your faith will grow weak.' My answer was to remain silent. At length I felt Christ was saying that my answer should be to witness; so I began to give my witness. Then there was lamenting in the city; people came from near and far to reason with me, but to no effect, for the light of faith had been kindled in my heart.

The day came when I decided it was necessary to enter into the world-wide fellowship of the church. I had learnt which was the true religion which gives salvation, so I was baptized in Shikarpur on July 15th 1967.

Before descending into the water my state of mind was very strange, such as I had never experienced before. It was nothing new to me to get into water, for I was a good swimmer, but this water was different. Before entering the water my heart was like a blossom just opening and coming into full bloom. On going under the water the second time I saw Christ's cross; I saw Christ himself taking me and uniting me with himself. I believe that Christ is God's Son, is God incarnate, who has saved me and has indeed saved the world by his own blood. One needs to be endowed with the riches of faith and then to know that one's sins have been washed away and personally to call Christ one's Lord and Saviour. This does not happen by arguments or by intellectual proof but by faith.

But black does not easily become white, as I know in my own experience. For a time I served in the Christian bookroom in Hyderabad, where plenty of young Muslims came to make enquiries and to read God's Word. My prayer is that my Muslim brothers will personally acknowledge that salvation is in Christ and that he is truly God's Son. The time will come when by the Holy Spirit's influence many people will recognize that Christ is the Saviour of the world.

5
I was forgiven

Some people feel that because Muslims believe in one God there is no need to preach the gospel to them. But I know that Christ has changed my life and I have found in him the peace I could not find elsewhere.

A sense of sin and the need to be forgiven weigh very heavily on some people. JOSEPH SEIDU MANS of Sierra Leone began to think deeply when an older Christian woman actually asked his forgiveness for a matter where he felt he was at fault. Not long after, he himself found forgiveness at the feet of Jesus and he has been his servant ever since. For some years he led the 'New Life for All' movement, and today he plays a leading part in the church in Sierra Leone and on a wider scale.

My parents were Muslims belonging to the Fulah or Fulani people. From my earliest days I was brought up in the Muslim faith, for my father was a leader in Islam. When I was only six years old I was sent away from my home town to a *karmoko* or Arabic teacher, with whom I stayed for about eight years. He taught me the Quran and the laws of Islam; I began to fast, to give alms, to offer sacrifice and to fulfil all the duties of a Muslim. In those days I knew nothing of Christianity, for there were no Christians in that area.

After I had twice been through the Quran, I went home; my father was planning to send me to his old home, Mamu in Guinea, but he died before he could carry out his plan. About this time I met some Christians who invited me to join their school. I was not interested in their religion, for I was quite convinced about Islam, but I did want to learn English and to get a modern education; so I accepted their invitation.

For five years I studied in this school before Christianity had any real effect on me. At that time I was living and working in the house of an elderly lady teacher. There were prayers in the home and Christian teaching was given; I even went to church on occasion, but was never convinced about the Christian faith.

One day the Governor came to the town (Kamabie), and the teacher entertained him to lunch. She asked me to wait at table, and I agreed; but later I angered her by refusing deliberately. The next morning when I went to work at the house, she refused to let me in; so I went off to school. I did not care about my bad behaviour.

In the afternoon I went to the house again. She was standing at the door and as I got close she called my name very softly and said, 'Seidu, forgive me.' I stood still for some time and then asked, 'What?' She said, 'I was vexed at you this morning.' I had never thought seriously about sin till then, but this made me wonder – why did she ask for my forgiveness, when I should have asked for her forgiveness because I had wronged her?

God used this humble asking for forgiveness on the part of that Christian woman to make me think very seriously about sin. This was the beginning of his wonderful way of bringing a sinner back to himself. Not long after that this dear old lady sent me to Gbendembu for further schooling. There God spoke to me in an evangelistic meeting, and even before the preacher had called us to pray I knelt down and confessed my sins to the Lord Jesus Christ. I felt that I was forgiven because there was peace in my heart and I was very happy.

But there was opposition immediately when I went back home. My uncles would not have me in the house, so I had to stay away for the next two years. After that they saw they could do nothing and noticed the great change in me. Before this incident I was a trouble-maker in the home. I fought a lot with many people, and several times they had been taken to court because of my bad behaviour. But after my conversion they saw none of this.

And so, being unable to persuade me to give up Christianity, they received me back in the home. As a result I able to bring my two brothers and my sister to the Lord Jesus Christ. I was not baptized for some three years, but when a new pastor came, he asked me about this. So I enrolled in the catechism (Christian instruction) class and was baptized.

For four years I was a teacher, and then I gave it up and entered the ministry, as God had spoken to me clearly about this. Then 12 years later in 1959 I felt God was leading me to a new kind of ministry requiring better education; so I went to the United States and studied in a college where I was able to challenge students about work overseas, a number of whom responded to the call.

I returned to Sierra Leone as a pastor and evangelist. In my church every member is concerned about evangelism; in the dry season we reach out to the villages around, so that now people come in from eleven villages up to a dozen miles away for Sunday worship. This year 65 people have been won to the Lord Jesus through the 'New Life for All' movement.

Some people feel that because Muslims believe in one God there is no need to preach the gospel to them. But I know that Christ has changed my life and I have found in him the peace I could not find elsewhere. I know that he is able to keep me from sinning and that he took care of me in trials and suffering when my relations forsook me.

In speaking to Muslims I start with what they know already, the creation, the fall, man's disobedience and the prophets. Then starting from Abraham we see God's promises about the Messiah. That leads on to the sinless life of Jesus and to the cross. Here I give my testimony, telling them that I am what I am today because of the cross, speaking of Christ's forgiveness and the power to conquer sin. I often speak in Christian secondary schools where there are Muslim students, many of whom have turned to Christ. When this happens they have to tell their parents, and in some cases the parents stop sending school fees; but the boys look to the Lord to provide the help they need in life.

6
The joy that I have found

That same day I heard the words, 'Come to me, all whose work is hard, whose load is heavy; and I will give you relief' (Matthew 11:28, NEB). That verse changed my life, for I was burdened down by the law and needed one to lean on.

For the devout person, consciousness of sin sometimes means living in fear. As a boy, JOHN PARWEZ was deeply absorbed in Islam. He gave much time to prayer and following the Sufi path. But this did not relieve his sense of sin and fear of hell. Then, in a Christian hospital, he heard the gospel of Jesus. His words promising relief to those who come to him changed John's life. He came to see that salvation is through God's free gift alone. God has helped him to face many trials and to humble himself. Now he is happily married and teaching at a school in a Christian village in Pakistan.

I belong to a Muslim family in Pakistan. From childhood I was interested in religious observances and had not merely a desire but an infatuation to learn about religion. I remember well that when I was only eight, people called me 'saint' and came to me for prayer, for they thought that whatever I uttered God would surely fulfil. When I went to school, I never fought with anyone but just got on with my study. I was not keen on games but was eager to associate with religious people. My family too was of a religious bent; my father was a learned and convinced Muslim, and I wanted to be like him so that people should respect me. So religious leanings reached the point of infatuation.

When I had passed the seventh class, my father fell ill and died. I stayed at school another year, but I was broken-hearted and lost interest in the world around me, preferring to remain alone. I left home and began to live in a desolate place, not caring about hunger and thirst and not returning home for weeks on end. Eventually a cousin of mine took me to a spiritual leader (a Sufi), to whom I swore allegiance as a disciple. He advised me to adopt spiritual asceticism; so I began to spend the nights without sleep in reading the Quran. Often I even forgot to eat and became very weak, so that I could scarcely walk. People began to come to me by day and night and to beg me to pray for them, so that they might obtain relief from illness, sickness and hardship. I had so lost interest in the world that I did not want anyone to come to me; but the more I wanted to escape from people, the more they pursued me.

Night and day I was engaged in observing the law of Islam, in the stated prayers, in private prayer, in vigils and so on. Yet I was also breaking the law and committing sins. Though I tried with all my might to do good actions, every day I committed some sin or other against God. The worst sin that I was guilty of was pride and conceit; for after worshipping God I thought that I was holy while everyone else was a sinner. I began to be very troubled, wondering how I could be set free from sin and thinking that without good actions I should surely go to hell. This fear was with me continually. I felt that I could not fulfil the law, which had become a heavy burden to me. At that time as a devout Muslim I had a long beard, but then I shaved it off completely, feeling that if I had given myself to God, what then was the need of appearances? My neighbours bègan to make objections, saying that the law was a matter of outward conduct – only God knows the heart. So as a Muslim I ought to follow the law, to pray and fast. I paid no attention to them, but remained very troubled in my mind.

At that time I had some eye trouble and had to go for treatment to the Taxila Christian Hospital, where I heard Christian preachers proclaiming God's Word. I listened with great attention, and their words led to the healing of my ills. That same day I heard the words, 'Come to me, all whose work is hard, whose load is heavy; and I will give you relief' (Matthew 11:28, NEB). That verse changed my life, for I was burdened down by the law and needed one to lean on. That verse forced me to go to talk things over with the preacher.

After my treatment I went home. I was now convinced of the truth of the Christian religion, but it was no light matter for me to forsake Islam. What would people say? What would the people who trust me think? My relations would revile me. This had been a great hindrance to me ever since I had heard the gospel message. I was in a great spiritual conflict and perplexity. But I kept on praying, 'Show me the right way. Give me the strength to follow him.' I was persuaded that the Lord Christ intercedes for the sinner and gives him comfort and peace.

Thanks be to God that he gave me courage, and I decided to go back to Taxila. There, some six months after I had received the Lord, I was baptized. At once I was sent away to Hyderabad for a course in the Bible. There I came to understand God's grace, revealed to me in Christ crucified, and his love made known to men through his Son. After this a desire for further education came to me, for I had only reached the eighth class. Now I am studying for a B.A. degree, and at the same time am bearing my witness for Christ in the presence of various people, chiefly Muslims, for I know that the Lord has chosen me especially for non-Christians. God gives me a wonderful power to bear witness and to share with others the joy which I have found through trusting Christ.

Since my conversion I have had to face many difficulties, but always the Lord has helped me and given me the victory over temptations. At first my family opposed me fiercely, but now they have come round and it is my great desire that somehow they may accept the Lord. Now I have been set free from all the bonds which the law imposes, and I rejoice that salvation is not by actions but by grace. God's Word tells us, 'There is no just man, not one' (Romans 3:10, NEB), and 'It is by his grace you are saved, through trusting him; it is not your own doing. It is God's gift, not a reward for work done. There is nothing for anyone to boast of' (Ephesians 2:8–9, NEB).

My life has completely changed. A spirit of service has taken the place of pride and conceit. After my conversion I have had to do very ordinary jobs: sweeping floors, washing dishes, acting as nightwatchman, and so on, and that without any distaste. This blessing has come to me through trusting Christ, who said, 'Among you, whoever wants to be great must be your servant, and whoever wants to be first must be the willing slave of all' (Mark 10:43–44, NEB).

Now I am teaching in an English-speaking school, and though on a low salary I am thoroughly happy. It is my ambition to enter a seminary to learn more about the Lord and to serve him better. I long that God's will may be fulfilled in my life and that I may go on bearing witness to what Christ has done for a sinner like me.

7
Everything became different

Repentance was what I needed! Repentance from regarding myself as the centre of the world . . . . By God's grace I gradually felt myself coming down to the place where I asked the Lord to have mercy upon me, a miserable sinner.

HASAN DEHQANI-TAFTI was brought up on the frontier of Islam and Christianity. He was drawn to Christ through the influence of his school. Some years later, at a time of deep inner discontent, he met with Christ in a new way through a fresh and deep repentance. In time he became Bishop of the Episcopal Church of Iran and showed tremendous courage in the face of personal danger and loss in the trials which assailed the Church following the Iranian revolution in 1979.

I was born and spent my childhood in Taft, a village near Yezd in central Iran. Through the Christian hospital at Yezd my mother had come to see the love of God revealed in Jesus and had been baptized, but the closing of the hospital in 1914 had obliged her to return to Taft and be married to a Muslim relative, Muhammad.

A Christian, Miss W A Kingdon, used to visit our home, where twenty or so would gather to hear her message. The death of my mother when I was five was a great tragedy for me, but God brought good out of that evil, as we shall see. I was brought up a Shiah Muslim and took part in the annual passion play representing the death of Hussain. But Miss Kingdon continually pressed my father to let me go to Yezd for education, for it was my mother's last wish that I should be brought up as a Christian. In the end my father took refuge in consulting the Quran, and the result came out as 'good'. When I was seven he was persuaded to let me go to the boys' school in the beautiful and historic city of Isfahan, the centre of Church Missionary Society work in Iran, with a college, schools and a hospital.

For a time I went through a kind of spiritual see-saw. For the first weeks of the summer holidays, I used to count myself a Christian, arguing with people about my beliefs; but within a few weeks the whole atmosphere of the village would influence me and turn me into a Muslim. By the time I was twelve the school influence had outweighed it and I had decided to be a Christian. In Taft I was more aggressively evangelistic than ever! So in response to pressure my father withdrew me from the school, but Miss Kingdon and Christian people in Isfahan urged him persistently to let me return. Again he consulted the Quran, and consented to my return. I made good progress at school.

At the age of 18 I was baptized and I wrote to my father, 'I have found the joy and happiness that I want in Jesus Christ.' When I returned to Taft on holiday I met much hostility and my own family regarded me as unclean, yet they were always loving and hospitable. In Isfahan I was given more responsibility in the church, reading the lessons, writing and translating hymns etc.; the unself-conscious happy zeal of those days is unforgettable.

In 1940 I left the college in Isfahan and was sent by the diocese to Tehran for higher education with a view to joining the ministry. Here I found myself in a secular atmosphere where philosophy and psychology were dominant. My simple faith had already been shaken during my last year at the college through studying elementary psychology; but there I was surrounded by wise Christian teachers. One of these advised me never to give up prayer and church-going, even if the whole thing seemed meaningless at times. I listened to this sound advice. In Tehran I found a helper in an American Christian with whom I could share my problems.

I graduated in 1943 and then had to undergo military training. I tried without success to obtain exemption, as I felt unable as a Christian to engage in war. I put down my religion as Christian, and the captain rebuked me severely when he found out that I had rejected my father's religion of Islam. After a while I was earning a good salary as a lieutenant, and my family had great hopes that I would raise their standard of living, but I remembered Christ's words, 'He who loves father or mother more than me is not worthy of me.' God had called me to ministry in the church, and I could not disobey the heavenly vision.

For two years after my discharge I was engaged in youth and Christian literature work. I was glad to serve the church, but inwardly I was not at rest and felt that I was failing to progress as a Christian. Then in 1947 I was sent to attend the World Christian Youth Conference at Oslo and to study at Ridley Hall, Cambridge.

The beauty and tranquility of Cambridge delighted me. But when the first excitement passed, the old restlessness of spirit cropped up again, this time in a more intense way. I was becoming lonelier and lonelier within myself. I blamed God for having taken my mother from me so early in my life, for deep down within myself I felt a vacuum for love – to be loved by someone for what I was, and not for what people would like me to be. The thought of a mother's warm bosom and a father's welcoming arms was so deep an unsatisfied desire with me, that thinking about it used to leave me cold and desolate. I blamed those who were the cause of my separation from my own people. The rush of the waves of self-pity and despair was sometimes so tremendous that they would press streams out of my eyes, and like Job I cursed the day I was born.

No-one seemed to understand me, or if they did I was

unable to be helped by them. Religious phrases such as 'surrender yourself to Christ', 'pray and he will grant you peace of mind' became for me mere clichés devoid of any real meaning.

In this situation I was put in touch with a Christian leader who had been able to help a number of young people through their difficulties. He listened to me for about two hours pouring my heart out to him with tears. I felt he loved and understood, and I was certain that through him I could be healed. In one of his talks with me he suggested that I should read the Psalms and the book of Job. The reading of these two books did to my difficulties what sunshine does to snow. All through Job I saw myself speaking:

'I loathe my life; I will give free utterance to my complaint... Why dost thou hide thy face, and count me as thy enemy?... Oh, that I knew where I might find him' (Job 10:1; 13:24; 23:3). In the end I found myself saying with Job: 'I had heard of thee by the hearing of the ear, but now my eye sees thee; therefore I despise myself, and repent in dust and ashes' (Job 42:5–6).

Repentance was what I needed! Repentance from regarding myself as the centre of the world. Now I saw myself as the sort of person I really was: a statue of selfishness, the essence of conceit, a perfect Pharisee. I had gone to England to become a better leader in our small church through good training and learning; but a Pharisee cannot learn, he must always teach! By God's grace I gradually felt myself coming down to the place where I asked the Lord to have mercy upon me, a miserable sinner.

When this happened everything became different. I knew what sin really was and what it cost God to forgive us through the cross of Jesus Christ. Once I started to know this and learn something of God's love, the healing came gradually. All worry, tension and restlessness began to vanish. I found I could even sleep better. People were no more difficult things to live with, but lovable and interesting persons who were the objects of God's love exactly as I was.

8

How can I be reconciled
to a holy God?

*It is often easier to approach people with God's message in
time of adversity, but I became a Christian at a time when in
worldly terms I was contented.*

When in prison for political reasons, MR NATHANAEL
IDAROUS of Zanzibar found a wonderful companion
– a New Testament. Gradually his understanding
grew until he turned to Christ as the one Saviour of
sinners. His family was greatly distressed, and it was
long before he could confess his faith in baptism. He
has found a deep joy and sense of fulfilment through
love for Jesus Christ.

From the age of five I was taught to read the Quran in
Arabic. At a place where great scholars of Islam have been
produced, I was a quiet student struggling to qualify as a
teacher of Islam, among the great towers from which the
melodious voices of the *muezzins* rang out, in an atmosphere
which did not encourage questioning. Luckily, however,
our tutor was a close relative of mine, and I belonged to a
Sharif family (supposed to be descendants of Muhammad),
thus enjoying a privileged position among Sunni Muslims.

In the 1964 revolution which overthrew the Sultan's
Arab rule in Zanzibar, I was detained for fourteen months
because of my political standing. With fifteen others, I was
confined in a cell about ten feet square; and here, one

bright cool morning, when the rain was dripping through the roof of the cell, I woke up to find a small book beside my rug. That was the first time I came across the New Testament. None of my cell-mates would own to it, so I assumed that a Red Cross visitor had placed it there. It proved a wonderful companion to me throughout the daytime which we used to spend outside the cell. Though still a Muslim I read it daily, and the more I read, the more I developed an attachment to it.

Then I came up against a question hard for Muslims to understand: 'How does one God exist in Trinity?' Though I felt unable for it, I decided to study Christ's mighty work and the extent of Muhammad's claim as a prophet. I was not prepared to doubt what was contained in the Bible, or to believe, as Muslims do, that Christians have changed the book of Christ. There was no-one to help me, for the only Christian there was the Prison Commissioner. But by God's grace, very soon after my detention, I was put in touch with Bible correspondence courses from Dar es Salaam and continued with these studies while going for Islamic lectures in the evening.

During this time I came to a fuller understanding of God's truth, until at last I received the gift of salvation through the redeeming blood of Jesus Christ. I made this decision through the clear guidance of God; it would take volumes to write all that I experienced. It is often easier to approach people with God's message in time of adversity, but I became a Christian at a time when in worldly terms I was contented. My conversion meant that I managed by God's grace to free myself from the bonds that restricted my knowledge of God. The Bible played a major part in it. From the beginning my heart was touched by two verses from the Epistles: one an announcement, 'For the grace of God has appeared for the salvation of all men' (Titus 2:11), and the other a challenge, 'How shall we escape if we neglect such a great salvation?' (Hebrews 2:3).

I read a number of books which were given to me, some of them pointing to particular denominations. But I decided that the Bible alone could give an answer to my thoughts and as a result I gradually lost interest in other books. Just at the right time I was presented with a Revised Standard Version of the Bible by the Principal of the Correspondence Institute, Mr Marston Martin, who later brought me together with a Christian community.

From the Bible I learnt that I was a sinner and all people are born with a sinful nature; this I realized was mankind's greatest problem. We read in 1 John 1:5–6, 'God is light and in him is no darkness at all. If we say we have fellowship with him while we walk in darkness, we lie and do not live according to the truth.' Here we see that all people are sinners, walking in darkness; but God is light, utterly different from mankind. Further, as light and darkness cannot live together, neither can God and sin. How can I who am a banished sinner be reconciled to a holy God? How can my sins be forgiven so that I can have fellowship with God? 'The saying is sure and worthy of full acceptance, that Christ Jesus came into the world to save sinners' (1 Timothy 1:15). Then this man Jesus whom I first took to be a prophet inferior to Muhammad was really the Saviour who came into the world to solve our greatest problem.

Among the hard-core Muslims of Zanzibar it was difficult for me to profess my faith in Christ. I knew how disappointed my mother would be, for whom our membership of the Sharif community was a precious gift from God. My elder brother's strong Marxist-Leninist convictions caused her deep distress; then came my detention to add to her affliction. My release was her one compensation, and she drew comfort from my continuance in the faith she had taught me.

A close friend was the first to notice that I kept away from the mosque, read the Bible often and went to church on Sundays. A family meeting was called to discuss the matter with me; I assured them of my love for the family and insisted that if there were objections to my being a Christian, my action should be discussed with reference to

40

its cause and the truth underlying it. Instead they decided to have a potion prepared with the Sheikh's blessing, believing that it had power to change my attitude. I could not refuse to take it from my mother's hands.

At the same time Christian friends were writing to me advising me not to fear to proclaim the Saviour's name. At the Martins' invitation I went for a fortnight to Dar es Salaam and there sought baptism, but the church elders would not baptize me without long preparation. There and in Kenya where I next went I enjoyed warm Christian fellowship with both African and European believers. Thence I went to Aden, my father's birthplace. It was a time of great tension and, living among Muslims, I could rarely meet my fellow Christians. A year passed before my baptism was agreed to. I insisted on its being by immersion, which presented difficulties in those disturbed times. In answer to my prayers this took place on the sea shore, thus symbolizing Christ's death, burial and resurrection as my own rising from the old nature into newness of life. Life has now come to its perfect adjustment with full love for Jesus Christ and with rejoicing night and day in my redemption through his blood. It is my earnest desire that every man and woman, girl and boy, may find the way of salvation and thus taste this sweet joy in Jesus Christ.

9
Pastor of all the town

'Weren't your parents pagans before you became Muslims? And did they force you to remain pagans? They allowed you to change to Islam because you believed that was right. If you force me to be a Muslim when my heart tells me to follow Jesus Christ, wouldn't that be a sin on your part?'

The kindly concern and love shown to all by a Christian worker drew TIMOTHY AKINLADE of Nigeria to the feet of Jesus Christ. Since then he has been able to win his father to share his faith, and serves today as a gifted pastor and evangelist in the Anglican Diocese of Ibadan.

Tiyamiyu Akinlade was born in 1935. His father was head of an important Muslim family group in his town. As a small boy Tiyamiyu was sent to study in the traditional Quranic school under the most learned teacher of the town; his father declared that he should never attend the ordinary primary school. But four years later when his father was away trading, other members of the family allowed Tiyamiyu to attend this school and by the time the father returned he had to accept the fact. But every evening after day-school was over he still attended the Quranic school, and by about 14 years of age he was familiar with the popular anti-Christian arguments; he had marked in his Bible the places where Moses gave instructions about performing ablution and where Jesus washed his disciples' feet, and again where Ezra 'acted as *muezzin* to call his people to prayer'. He would use these verses to attack Christians, claiming that they should be performing ablution and ritual prayer as Muslims do.

The local church worker made friends with the father, however, and in return Tiyamiyu would play with the boys at the mission house and would notice all that went on. He saw this man's kindly concern for all his visitors; chatting, entertaining, inquiring into their welfare and offering help. In contrast to this he saw people coming to his Quranic teacher for magical practices. Sometimes they wanted protection against evil, sometimes they asked for magic to do evil to others. Tiyamiyu felt his teacher was out to make profit and cared little about the people's welfare.

So Tiyamiyu thought more and more about the Christian message. He began to love the Bible. Soon he wanted to be a Christian; but he did not dare speak of this to his father. He managed to spend a year with his Christian friend in another place. Back at home again he was appointed teacher in a Muslim primary school. Here he had to perform Muslim prayers and attend the mosque 'in body but not in spirit'. On Sunday he dared not attend church at home, but visited a Christian relative some miles away in order to attend church there. He told the minister of that church that he wanted to be baptized, and he was secretly baptized there just after his nineteenth birthday, changing 'Tiyamiyu' to 'Timothy'.

Soon his father heard the news, called a meeting of the family, and announced that next Friday he would take Timothy to the mosque to wash off his baptism and make him a Muslim again! Timothy listened meekly to their discussion, but eventually managed to make his point: 'Weren't your parents pagans before you became Muslims? And did they force you to remain pagans? They allowed you to change to Islam because you believed that was right. If you force me to be a Muslim when my heart tells me to

43

follow Jesus Christ, wouldn't that be a sin on your part?'

The family was angry, but accepted the inevitability of the young man's decision. He got a job as a teacher, began Christian training and finally graduated from Immanuel Theological College at Ibadan in 1967. The family was by now somewhat reconciled; he was able to visit his home, but he could not say a word to any member of the family about his Christian faith, and he had to contribute money for the celebration of some Muslim festivals.

In 1967 Timothy was due to become a Christian minister. With much persuasion his father was brought to the cathedral to see his son ordained. Timothy was chosen to read the Gospel, and helped to serve the elements at the holy communion. Afterwards his father said, 'What were you giving to one another there?' Timothy replied, 'I can't explain it to you now, but I will pray that one day you will be a participant.' This service was the first time his father had been present at Christian worship. Somehow God spoke to him there; somehow he saw the glory of God there, for next week he said, 'I am going to church with you', and from that time he told the world that he was a follower of Jesus Christ. Several younger members of the family have also trusted Christ, but Timothy's mother is still a devout Muslim today. On visiting her son the first thing she asks is, 'Will there be a place for me to perform the prayers?'

For the first few years after his conversion Timothy did not want to hear anything about Islam. It was simply the religion he had rejected. He closed his mind to it – why bother about such a thing? So he was surprised when, at the end of his theological college course, he was asked to attend a four-month course in Islamic studies. There he learnt not only to read and translate some sections of the Quran, but also developed a more sympathetic under-standing of Islam and Muslims.

When he went as a minister to his first church, he found it in the throes of a bitter controversy, but with patience the members were reconciled. From the first he showed that he was just as much interested in the Muslims of the small town as he was in the Christians. The Muslims knew him as a convert and were ready to be suspicious and defensive. So, wisely, he did not discuss Islam, but visited them as much as he visited the Christians and devoted himself to anything to do with the common welfare. He took a hoe to help in road making; he helped found a maternity clinic, so that the townsfolk need no longer travel eight miles to clinic; he encouraged the establishment of a fish farm where young men could find employment; he regularly called on the chief and his counsellors at the palace. People began to say, 'This is not the Christians' pastor but the pastor of all the town.' Yet he would not join in Muslim ceremonies which might involve compromise of his Christian faith. 'You know how to say the *Fatiha* (the opening chapter of the Quran). Say it with us!' Muslims sometimes said. But he would reply discreetly, 'Let's discuss that another time, please.'

On one occasion a new chief of the town was enthroned. He was a Muslim, and soon he went on pilgrimage to Mecca. While he was there, the most fanatical of the Muslims went round the town, entered the compounds of the pagans and forcibly destroyed their objects of worship. Their aim was that, whereas previous Muslim chiefs had observed traditional pagan ceremonies, they would force the new chief to practise a pure Islam – there would be no paganism left for him to compromise with. Then, they believed, the pagans would be forced to turn to Islam. But what happened was quite different! In the end it was joy to the Christians and glory to Jesus Christ. Persecuted by Muslims, the pagans would never accept Islam; in little groups they started coming to church. That year twenty-six adults were baptized, five Muslims, twenty-one pagans. The Muslims said proverbially, 'We have drained the pond, but the Christians are catching the fish!'

After that Timothy served the 'Islam in Africa' project before going on to university studies in Islamics. He has a warm, happy, optimistic temperament. He loves music and drama, and uses them in the service of the gospel. He encourages Muslims to explain their religious outlook, seeking first to understand people and really to listen to what they say. When the time comes to give his own witness to Christ, he knows how to set his hearer at ease, how to speak plainly without causing offence. Rather than speaking to crowds he recommends the quiet talk with one Muslim or a few. Many Christians today question whether they should witness to Muslims. Timothy is in himself a living answer to that question!

10
The giver of salvation and peace

This book has great power. I want to see it do for others what it has done for me.

The name of 'martyr' is often claimed for those who do not deserve it, who died through their own rashness or in defence of some other cause than God's. But the list of Christian believers who forsook Islam includes many true martyrs, many of them unknown and unbaptized. ESTHER JOHN was drawn by the life of a Christian teacher to study the Bible, where she found Jesus as the living Saviour. Some years later in Pakistan her life was cut short by the hand of an unknown assassin.

'When I was about seventeen, I was studying in the eighth class of a government school in South India. Then, because of my father's illness, I had to leave school for a while. After some time I was sent to a Christian school near my home. Just as soon as I set foot in this school, I noticed a Christian teacher who was different from anyone I had ever known. I saw her gentle way of speaking, her kindness to all the students and her great faithfulness in her work. Her life made so deep an impression upon me that I was really puzzled. "How could any human being be like that?" I wondered over and over again. Later I realized that it was all because God's Spirit was in her.

'In this school I began to study the Bible. Two days in the week we studied the Old Testament and two days the New Testament. One day we did memory work, learning passages from the Bible and many songs. At first I did not study with zeal but rather indifferently. I had heard Christians called blasphemers and I did not like even to touch their book.

'One day we were studying the 53rd chapter of Isaiah, memorizing some parts of it, which was very hard for me. It was while studying this chapter that God, by his grace, showed me that there was life and power in this book. Then I began to realize that Jesus is alive for ever. Thus God put faith in my heart and I believed in Jesus as my Saviour and the forgiver of my sins. Only he could save me from everlasting death. Only then did I begin to realize how great a sinner I was, whereas before I thought that my good life could save me.

'Now a living power began to work in me. When Satan would try to catch me with his nets and chains, I could resist him by reading the New Testament and trusting Christ. Now for Jesus' sake I had to leave my home and loved ones. He took me to Christian friends who gave me a home. After some time I was baptized. Then I could say with a full faith that Jesus is the giver of salvation and peace. Such peace the world cannot give; it is the gift of God.'

This is a brief personal record written by Esther. Her former name was Qamar Zea. She came to Karachi from South India soon after the partition of India in 1947. A Christian worker, to whom a friend in South India had written about her, sought her out and was surprised by her grace and beauty. In the brief time that they could speak together in private, Qamar asked Miss Laugesen to bring her a New Testament at night. Miss Laugesen left Karachi for a time, and they did not meet till seven years later, when Qamar came to her, having left her home where her marriage was being planned. That little New Testament, read in secret, had kept her faith alive without the help of any human being. Her relations came to plead with her, and she went back for a few days to see her mother.

When she returned, she was sent north to Sahiwal in the Punjab, to live in the nurses' home at the Christian Hospital. Here she enjoyed the happy companionship of other Christian girls and studied the faith in preparation for baptism, at which she took the name Esther John. She played a full part in the life of the hospital and was thrilled when she could do the simplest service for others or take part in the work of evangelism.

In 1956 she went to the United Bible Training Centre at Gujranwala, where she proved to be an apt student with an inquiring mind which could not be satisfied with superficial solutions. She gained an insight into Scripture and a skill in handling it that would put many life-long Christians to shame. She loved the Bible and even before her baptism had said, 'I feel God wants me to be a teacher of the Bible. This book has great power. I want to see it do for others what it has done for me.' During one summer vacation at Sahiwal, she had a period of serious illness, which was a time of testing for her. After tears and questionings, God gave her victory and she was restored to complete health.

In 1959, having completed her course, she moved to the little town of Chichawatni, where a Christian worker, Mrs Dale White, invited Esther to take over her guest-room and to become her colleague. Here she settled down happily in the shady, well-watered compound with its brightly flowering trees. 'Chichawatni is my lovely home', she would say. She adopted the Punjabi dress with its baggy trousers in place of the Indian *sari*, and she struggled with the Punjabi language, which she never quite mastered. She had learnt to cycle, a rare accomplishment for women in Pakistan, and many eyes would turn when she and Mrs White, an elderly American who had spent most of her life in the Punjab, set off to visit the town or a neighbouring village.

Together they entered Muslim homes, to which the custom of seclusion often restricted the women for the greater part of their lives. They soon recognized her as coming from a Muslim background, and once one said, 'You still have the light of the holy Prophet Muhammad in your face!' But when Esther went to tell her story and to speak of Jesus the Messiah, admiration gave way to puzzlement and hostility. Often they asked her, 'How could you do it?', and she would reply, 'God's grace was upon me.' Then she would tell the good news of Jesus in story, picture and song, and people would often listen, fascinated. Sometimes she was met with mocking and reviling, but this did not trouble her.

When the hot summer gave place to cool winter she joined the Whites in their camps in the villages. For five or six days they would stay in one spot to give basic Bible teaching to the little Christian congregation of very poor and mostly illiterate people. Esther delighted to identify herself with them and to accompany their songs with the rhythmic beating of her drum. She would join the cotton-pickers in the fields and find joy in the beauty of the countryside. They were back in the little town for Christmas, and Esther threw herself into training the children to present a beautiful Christmas drama.

Those were happy days, but she was a little uneasy as her family were pressing her in frequent letters to return home. She packed her trunk and was intending to leave at the end of the year. But she had no peace of mind about this. After much prayer she sat down and wrote a letter giving two conditions for her return: that she be allowed to live as a Christian and that she should not be forced into marriage. The letter went by registered mail, but no answer came.

She was away for another month camping with her Christian friends, then came back with them to Chicha-watni, where the pastors and evangelists from the area were to assemble for their monthly meeting. That evening she was busy in her room, polishing her pots and pans and happily singing to herself. She went to bed early having a slight cold. At night the house was full of guests; yet somehow an enemy managed to creep in while all were sleeping. In the morning she did not appear. She was found dead in her bed, her skull smashed in with some heavy, sharp instrument.

Her body was laid to rest in the Christian cemetery at Sahiwal. Muslims joined with Christians in the funeral service, which included the triumphant words, 'Be thou faithful unto death, and I will give thee a crown of life.' Police took charge of the house and laboriously went through all her books and papers seeking a clue, perhaps a note from a disappointed lover. In the end they reported to the master of the house, 'Sir, we have found no clue. This girl was in love only with your Christ.' A beautiful chapel in the grounds of the Christian Hospital at Sahiwal, for use of staff and patients, is a fitting tribute to her memory.

11
I will serve him all my life

The colour of my past was black and its smell was of alcohol, women and sin. The colour of my present is light, covered with joy and peace from the source of all peace, Jesus.

MR AHMAD SOUSSI, a young Moroccan, rebelled from the restraints of home and slipped into a life of crime. He was amazed by the forgiveness of a Christian, who was one of his victims. Later he read the New Testament and was gripped by the message of Christ's love, forgiveness and salvation. His family cast him out, but after some time, seeing his changed life, were reconciled to him. Since then he has helped in Christian radio programmes and studied at a Bible School. Today he is serving his Lord in his own land of Morocco.

Leaving the small village where I was born, I travelled to Casablanca to continue my studies in a secondary school, to live with my uncle and to help him in his business; I was 17 years old. In the city I followed the crowd. It was not very difficult to recognize street girls and men; I made their acquaintance and soon became one of them. I failed my exams and reaped what I had sown.

Once my uncle's wife saw on my table a picture of me with some girls. My uncle wrote to my father to come soon. My father asked me where I had been passing my time. I replied, 'Playing soccer.' My father showed me the picture with the girls and cried, 'Go away, you perverse son. You are not worthy of me as your father.'

I left the house and walked the streets without any destination. One of my old friends came and asked me to tell him what had happened. I told him everything. He said, 'Did you forget that I passed the same way five years ago? In spite of that I am not discouraged. Now I am free from my parents' authority!'

I exclaimed, 'Do you think by being lost you are free?'

'Call it what you like,' he said. 'The essential thing is that I find a piece of bread and a place to sleep. In our country we cannot find more than that. If I am lost, you are lost. Then come with me and meet the leader of our gang and work with us.' He persuaded me because I had nothing to eat and no work.

The head of the band trained me how to steal. I spent seven months at this and made enough money to eat, smoke and drink. But the police found our hide-out, and once again I was on the street. One of my friends and I then worked as delivery boys in the vegetable market. We took a lady's purse from her basket and were soon arrested and taken to the police station. We confessed having taken the money and returned to her what was left. When the policeman asked if she wanted to press charges, she said, 'No, I want to forgive them because Jesus forgave me and forgives everyone his sins.'

These words touched my heart and continued to speak to me. Who is Jesus? Why does he forgive? Why did the lady forgive us? Many questions without answers passed through my thoughts at that time.

The law does not forgive as Jesus forgives. So I spent seven months in prison. My father knew I was there, and when I was released, he met me. With tears in my eyes I asked his forgiveness, and received it.

The following year my father arranged to enrol me in a Quranic school. I agreed in order to please him. During this year I read many history books, especially about the

Roman occupation of North Africa. I understood that the religion of our ancestors before Islam came was Christianity. The Muslim armies had forced the people to embrace their religion; that was why we were Muslims. Doubt filled my heart and I stopped praying because praying had never given me spiritual satisfaction. I was considered irreligious, so I left the school.

Soon after, I returned to Casablanca at my uncle's invitation. There I met someone from the Middle East called Kamel who owned a restaurant. Once when I asked his opinion about religion he replied, 'You know, Ahmad, I am a Christian and not a Muslim as you think.'

'But you are an Arab', I said. 'Are there Christians among the Arabs?'

'You forget that the Middle East was an area of many Christian tribes and kingdoms. You in North Africa think that the only Christians are Europeans and this is not the truth.' Then he gave me a New Testament to read.

At home in my room I closed my door and started reading it. The first thing that struck me was that the gospel was in Arabic and its message was valid for everyone of any race. I knew with assurance that Jesus said, 'I will never turn away anyone who comes to me.'

I visited Kamel another time and he asked me if I had read the book and what I thought about it. I replied that I had and was touched by the many sentences of love in the New Testament. Kamel said, 'What about salvation? Did you read that anyone who believes in Christ will be forgiven his sins?'

I knew the addresses of Bible correspondence schools and many courses were sent to me. They helped to open my eyes to the truth that God is light and there is no darkness at all in him. Then I began Bible studies with a brother in Christ, to deepen my knowledge of God's Word.

One evening after supper I went to a meeting, unaware that a neighbour was following me, sent to watch me by my uncle. Between my present and my past there is a great difference. The colour of my past was black and its smell was of alcohol, women and sin. The colour of my present is light, covered with joy and peace from the source of all peace, Jesus. But my uncle did not recognize the difference. When I returned from the meeting, he attacked me and the next morning took me to the police station with a neighbour.

The police officer asked what I had stolen, since most complaints involved theft. 'He has not stolen anything,' my uncle began, 'but what he has done is far more serious and must be made public. He has denied his religion. I only wish he had stolen something; that would be nothing by comparison.'

'You have nothing to do with his religion and his faith', said the police officer. 'If he works honestly, he is free to think as he chooses. This is not the concern of the authorities.' So he let us go.

Disappointed, my uncle encouraged the neighbours to give me the isolation treatment and insult me. The only consolation in my heart was from the words of the gospel. A few days later I was called before a council; which included my father and uncle, a neighbour, three religious leaders and some others. Before entering the room I prayed that God would give me courage and he reminded me, 'The Holy Spirit will teach you in the same hour what you ought to say.'

One of the religious leaders opened the meeting, addressing me: 'Listen, my friend, don't accept another religion. Don't be tempted to change because the consequences are very serious.'

I waited till the end of his talk and said, 'Listen, my friends. You have heard of Jesus, the Spirit of God, and of his miracles: he healed the sick, he stilled the storm, he raised the dead, he lived a sinless life, he died on the Cross, he himself was raised from the dead, he ascended into heaven and he will come back. Do you want to believe in him?'

Everyone stared at me in amazement, while the religious leader angrily slapped me, saying, 'How can you abandon the religion of your parents and grandparents?'

'Faith does not come as an inheritance from one's parents,' I replied, 'it is the result of the Holy Spirit's work. Physically I am always my father's son, but spiritually I am a child of God. He delivered me from sin's slavery. How can you want me to return to that bondage?'

The religious leader cried loudly to everyone present, 'I warn you, anyone who eats or sleeps under the same roof with an infidel like this will be an infidel just as he is.'

So I found myself in the street for a third time without work or a home. I thought of a friend, a carpenter, and I went to see him. I stayed with him for many days. My friend was touched by my testimony and later believed in the Lord Jesus as his Saviour.

During this time I never stopped praying for work. One day I heard a voice behind me, 'Ahmad, come here.' It was Brahim, my father's friend, an important businessman in the city. 'I want to ask about your family', he said.

'My family is well. That's all the news I've had for months.'

'Why?'

'They've kicked me out of the house because of my religion, and now I am looking for work.'

'I need someone. If you want to, you can work for me.'

'Thank you very much, but you must know that I have become a Christian.'

'I didn't ask you about your religion. If you are clever and honest, that's all I require.'

I thanked the Lord and began work the next day. Days, weeks and months passed. All the customers appreciated my work and the way in which I dealt with them. Seven months later Brahim had to go away on business and left me in charge of the shop. When he returned, he invited me to his house, saying, 'Here's some money. Go and get a haircut and dress up and come to supper with us.'

What a surprise awaited me when I entered his home. There were my father, mother and aunt. Returning from his journey Brahim had passed through my village and brought back my family. I threw myself in my parents' arms and they kissed me with tears. Then, instead of reproaching me, my father leaned towards me and whispered, 'Ahmad, forgive me, my son, for my previous behaviour. Your uncle in the past told me much about you and I thought you were like the young scoundrels who walk the streets, living with women and taking drugs. I was saddened by these reports, but when Brahim told me about you recently, I was so happy.'

'Yes, father, I was what you thought I was. Now Jesus has taught me a great deal and has brought me into his sheepfold because I was a lost sheep. I believe in him and I will serve him all my life. Let us turn over a new page in our lives.'

12
The pearl of great price

It is not what a man gives up but what he finds that really counts. Had I a thousand lives to offer, I would offer all to Christ.

DR M ABDUL QAYYUM DASKAWIE of Pakistan comes from a devout Muslim family of high intellectual calibre. His involvement in the politics of national liberation interrupted his studies at college, but he continued his reading, and almost by chance began to study the New Testament and found the message of a God of love, of a God who was like a forgiving father, deeply attractive. His visits to a Christian, to enquire further, caused such a violent reaction from his family that he had to leave home. So he determined to become a Christian, and this he did through great hardship. Later he had a distinguished career as an educationist and a church leader, earning the respect of all communities.

I was born at Sialkot in 1903 of a family which claimed descent from the Quresh, who ruled Mecca at the time of Muhammad. My uncle was a distinguished scholar who wrote the first dictionary of Urdu, as well as a number of books, pamphlets and poems. He was very zealous for his faith and much in demand as a speaker at religious meetings. My father taught at Sialkot, then worked for some years at

Ludhiana, returning to Sialkot during the troubled days of 1919. There I studied at the mission college, Murray College, which had a high reputation for discipline and the quality of its staff. Here there was Bible teaching, but we would either quietly slip out when the teacher closed his eyes for prayer after roll-call or stay to ask uncomfortable questions.

In those days there was a great upsurge of political activity, with the demand for political emancipation and great agitation among the Muslim students over the abolition of the *Khilafat*, through the deposition of the *Caliph*, the Sultan of Turkey. I was affected by the general unrest and decided not to pursue my studies at college. No-one could persuade me to change my mind.

Now I had plenty of time for reading, and I looked through my uncle's library. In it I came across a book of Urdu poetry written by him, called 'A True Christian's Prayer'. I was surprised to see it and immediately sat down to read it. Its main argument was the traditional one that the Christians having gone astray, the Muslims were now the true successors to their faith. In this role my uncle pleaded with Christians to accept his faith. It had footnotes with references to the Christian Scriptures which I began to look up in my father's New Testament, a present from the British and Foreign Bible Society. I also read some of the verses before and after each reference, and thus came across some of the parables, miracles and teachings of the New Testament. What I read puzzled me; I could not understand the great differences between what I believed and what was in the gospel. I was particularly impressed by what was said about God and his relation to man. How could there be a God who would wait for the return of a prodigal son? And in any case how could God be a father to man?

Such problems agitated my mind. If I mentioned them to anyone in the family, I knew I would get into serious trouble. I sought the help of a Christian classmate, who took me to the Rev. R McCheyne Paterson, a man of eminent piety and learning. We talked for some time and agreed to meet again.

As my study continued I was entranced especially by the idea of a God of love, a love all-embracing, pure and holy, absolutely different from the love that was so much talked of in our circles; but its full significance was beyond me. The Sermon on the Mount with its simple yet baffling statements was even more bewildering. But the things which at this stage I could not accept were the Trinity and the atonement. I did not desire to doubt the faith of my fathers, but I was attracted by this new philosophy of life.

About this time I went to a Muslim religious fair near Sialkot to which people came from all over the country. I wanted to see what brought so many people to the shrine. I sat among the worshippers listening to a long address. I had no evening meal, but slept soundly on a bare string bed, till wakened by the morning call to prayer. Then I caught the train and arrived home hungry and tired. I ate something and immediately fell asleep.

How long I slept I do not know, but I was awakened by a shock. My father had heard of my visits to Mr Paterson and instead of talking to me about it, he beat me and told me I was on my own from that time onward. The main reasons for this violent reaction were the terrible shock it gave to our family pride as religious leaders and the attitude of Islam itself towards those who question its tenets. A cousin said, 'You were once my brother; now you are an enemy.' My money and keys had gone. My aunt sat up late into the night, bathing my wounds and bruises.

Now that I was cut off from my family, any hesitation I had about my faith in Christ came to an end. I went to Pasrur, where I stayed with a friend and went to see the local Christian leader, the Rev. J G Campbell. He knew my father and realized I could not be baptized in Pasrur or Sialkot; so he sent me to Landhaur, 500 miles away in the United Provinces. I travelled twenty-four hours by train, and then climbed some 4,000 feet up the mountain side, arriving tired and hungry. I was given a room and sat down on the bed. Night had come and it was very cold; so I matched my faith against the cold and the thinnest of covering, waiting for the dawn. There was no light to cheer me, but I was filled with an unspeakable joy which kept me warm. Later I must have dozed off; for when I opened the door to a knock, the sun was coming over the hillside. My visitor was the doctor to whom I was to teach Urdu. In the afternoon another teacher provided me with food, the first for thirty-six hours.

I was baptized on May 1st 1921, seven weeks before my 18th birthday. In the autumn, arrangements were made for me to resume my studies, this time at Rawalpindi, returning to Landhaur the next summer. The following Christmas I was left alone in the boarding-house, having nowhere to go. On Christmas Day I returned alone to my room after church, having no money and no invitation for a meal. A hostel servant kindly lent me sixpence, so I had threepence for lunch and the same for supper. Late in the evening there was a tap at my window. One of the Indian professors had brought some cakes and fruit. 'My wife has sent these,' he said. In the whole city there was only one person who had given me a thought! This friendly gesture led to a friendship which became more precious with the years.

My father was reconciled to reality when he discovered that I really meant to be a Christian. He had refused to help me 'because I was a Christian', but now he was even proud that I had done well.

Most people, after reading this account, will ask whether all this loneliness, privation and suffering had been worthwhile. In other words, what have I gained by becoming a Christian? In the first place, it is not what a man gives up but what he finds that really counts. Would you have offered condolences to the merchant in Jesus' parable who was rejoicing over his great find? I am the man whose ploughshare turned up the treasure and the merchant who was looking for the pearl. The good life in Christ, the knowledge of God that he has brought, and the indestructible hope that he has given me, more than compensate for any trouble I have suffered.

Christ is the pearl of great price – the best, the purest and the highest the world has ever known. Had I my life to live again I would not make it any different in this respect; and had I a thousand lives to offer, I would offer all to him. The knowledge of a God who loves and who is 'Abba, Father' is beyond belief but true. I know of nothing higher or better.

To me the marvel of marvels is the story of a God who dared to be *man*, yes, man enough to stoop down to my level to love me to manhood. How wonderful is the heritage which is ours in Christ! He is 'the crystal-clear Christ', who lies open to the closest scrutiny. He has nothing to hide, no dark chapters in his life, no ulterior motives, no reservations. He is transparently clear in love and service of others. 'Others he saved, himself he would not save.' Loyal and steadfast even to the death on the cross.

In the whole range of human history I cannot find anyone so noble, so pure, so far-sighted, so generous and forgiving as he. The best people I know are most like him. Would the world not be heaven itself if there were more like him? No wonder from the beginning people worshipped him as divine. He is the telescope focused on God to bring the divine radiancy within reach of mortal men and women.

When the world finally achieves sanity, it will be on his terms. He is the goal of humanity as well as the goal of history. He has brought a new outlook on life, new insight, new hope. Though I fall so far short of anything that he is and anything he tells me to do, he is still the highest that I adore and long for. There is the assurance that by his help, by the transforming power of his fellowship we shall achieve it.

'Without the glass the colour of wine you cannot see,
    Though with the wine the glass itself shall hidden be;
So every act of Christ the invisible God portrays,
    To all the world divine effulgence he displays.'

13
A total self-awakening

I became a Christian because I was confronted with God's love in Christ. What I experienced after that, and continue to experience, is more than I ever expected or dreamt of.

A. RAZZAQ BARAKAT ULLAH of Mauritius is one of those who came to a living faith through agonizing doubt and painful heart-searching. In this condition a little book presented Jesus Christ to him as the Saviour of men. Many questions arose in his mind, but God's love in Christ confronted him and he became a new person, accepting himself, rejoicing in God's love and enriched by new friendships.

My parents were devout Indian Muslims living in Mauritius, who strictly obeyed the law of Islam. I learnt to read and write Urdu and to read the Quran (though without understanding), and then went to an Islamic secondary school, where there was much emphasis on Islamic history, culture and theology. I carried out the religious duties, but gradually came to question their relevance. I had been told that only through them could I win Paradise in the hereafter, and I was anxious about whether I would gain God's mercy or his displeasure. My soul sought a solace which neither the prayers nor fasting nor reading the Quran could bring. I resolved to get to the very core of Islam, behind the traditions, and for that there was nothing but the Quran.

So I began to read it in a French translation.

All Muslims believe that the proof of the divine origin of the Quran lies in its surpassing beauty, and this I had experienced when listening to professional reciters in the mosque or on the wireless. But when I came to read it in French I was puzzled and disappointed by its contents, which seemed full of repetitions and dire threats. My faith was more severely shaken by chapter 33, where I read how Muhammad, by special revelation, married the wife of Zaid his adopted son, when he already had nine wives. There seemed to be a different standard for him and for other believers.

At the age of sixteen I reflected on these passages, and months of doubts and painful heart-searching followed. Granted the beauty of the Arabic Quran, this was not enough proof of its divine origin. I pondered too the triumph of Islam – surely the hand of God was with them! But Communism has spread in the last fifty years so as to dominate the lives of a third of mankind. So the debate went on in my mind, and I gave up the fast and the prayers, except for the Friday prayers on which my father insisted.

Some months later I was sitting by my father in the mosque and reflecting – Do Paradise and hell exist? Is there life after death? Don't we just get snuffed out when we die? Then I thought, 'Surely the best way to serve God is to serve my fellow men.' I had already decided to study medicine; there and then I dedicated myself to alleviating the sufferings of others. Later I realized that this would involve much personal self-sacrifice and self-denial, but I found in myself the same self-centredness and greed which I saw in others. The future always held a certain anxiety for me – Will I be a failure or a success in life? Or will I always linger in mediocrity? Further, I was troubled with a sense of inferiority, heightened by a bad stammer; so I studied hard to prove myself and show I was better than my classmates. I thought, 'If I can get a first grade in O level, I'll be happy.' I got what I wanted, but the sense of achievement and elation I expected eluded me. It was the same at A level. Then I thought, 'I'll finally achieve happiness when I get to fabulous Britain. I'll be a university student, with plenty of money, master of my own life.'

I left home in 1963, sad at leaving my parents but full of expectation. The thrill of being in a new country soon wore off, with the cold wet climate, the difficulty of finding rooms, the strangeness of everything. There was no-one to whom I could turn. I had to attend lectures in vast halls among hundreds of students; it was all so impersonal. I was alone all the time; desperately alone in the midst of a noisy bustling crowd. I sought friends and fellowship and met only with politeness. I was so depressed that I went to see the dean and told him I was giving up medicine. He cautioned me against any hasty decision and told me that first-year medicine is always depressing. So I held on, wondering, 'Will I ever achieve peace and serenity? Or is happiness just a will o' the wisp?'

One morning in this mood I met Jim Swanney outside the lecture theatre. Once acquainted, we met often and had long chats together about politics and other aspects of life. His attitude was positive and confident, dominated by a vital faith in God. Others just lived for the weekends, and their lively accounts of weekend fun left me scandalized and disgusted. Much time was spent in bed; the rest mostly in boozing and wenching, followed by a hang-over and an 'awful Monday morning feeling'. I thought, 'What a caricature of what life ought to be!' But my life was hardly any better. I did not know how to live life fully and deeply.

Once Jim introduced me to the youth fellowship of his church, and I was again impressed how different and cheerful they were. When I asked one of them the reason, he told me that their having Jesus Christ as Saviour and Lord made all the difference. I had no idea what he meant; further, I thought it strange that sensible people could believe that God had a son, Jesus Christ, just like a man. But my curiosity in the Christian faith was aroused. Jim gave me a New Testament in the Authorized Version, but I found the old English difficult and irritating, so gave it up after a few chapters.

Then one Saturday in May 1965 I went to a meeting organized by the Christian Union; I do not remember much of the address, but I picked up a booklet entitled *The Crux of Christianity*. Returning home I casually began to read it.

The writer expounded mankind's rebellion against God which has alienated us from him, so much that we can do nothing to put ourselves right with God. Our relationship with him becomes one of law instead of love. God could not forcibly reconcile us to himself, for he wants human beings, not robots, for his sons. Nor could he ignore our rebellion or just leave us to perish; for he loves us every one. Faced with this predicament he did the unimaginable, yet the only thing. He himself came down to mankind as the man Jesus of Nazareth; he identified himself totally with humanity and allowed the sin of men and women to prevail against him. Executed as a common criminal on a trumped-up charge, he was bearing the fearful consequences of our sin. In so doing God demonstrated once and for all his love for people and his judgment upon sin. In the person of Jesus he shows us his forgiveness and invites us to be reconciled to him. 'Now,' the writer asked, 'what is your response to this love? How would you feel if your love and care were spurned?'

The last few years came before me and I saw God's love and guiding hand. He had answered my prayers in times of trouble and I had soon forgotten about him. I remembered my opposition to Jesus Christ and how I had once taken bread and wine in mockery of the Lord's Supper. Yet he had continued to love me and care for me. I had no alternative but to kneel down and ask for his forgiveness.

After a rather agitated night I went to church, as it was Sunday, preoccupied with thoughts about my parents' likely attitude to the disgrace my conversion would bring upon the family. How could I do this to them, whom I loved very dearly? What would happen to my career, when I was dependent on my father for every penny? My Christian friends told me that I must cast all my care upon Christ, who would give me strength; but they had no idea of the nature of my problem. Gradually I learnt what it is to have faith in God, and as I experienced his grace in Christ I became bolder in my witness, so that all my countrymen in Glasgow knew about it. Soon I began to ask a lot of questions about the faith: the reliability of the New Testament, the meaning of Jesus' Sonship and death, the Trinity, and so on. I had to satisfy myself that Christianity is reasonable; there is no place for mental laziness. I had to try to understand the faith and to relate it to living in the modern world.

I became a Christian because I was confronted with God's love in Christ. What I experienced after that, and continue to experience, is more than I ever expected or dreamt of. I have come to know God as the Father who loves me and cares for me, not just from what Jesus taught but from how he dealt with unlovable people like Zacchaeus (Luke 19) and the Samaritan woman (John 4).

So I came to seek God's will for me and to strive by his enabling grace to accomplish it. I pray not just to obtain things, but because communion with God is sweet, refreshing and renewing. Because of the assurance that God loves me and accepts me as I am, I learnt to accept myself as I am. Thereby I entered into a thrilling experience of discovering myself. Abilities and potentials which I had only glimpsed before came to the surface and to fruition. My inferiority complex went away and my stammer became hardly perceptible.

Conversion has been for me a total self-awakening, spiritual, emotional and intellectual. I have embarked on many deep and satisfying friendships. I used to be conscious among Europeans and Africans of my race and colour; but now among Christians of any race I have no racial consciousness at all. This marvel of Christian fellowship was so tremendous that I kept seeking the cause of it. The answer I found in St Paul (Ephesians 2:11–16, NEB): 'But now in union with Christ Jesus you who once were far off have been brought near through the shedding of Christ's blood. For he is himself our peace.' Whenever I meet a Christian who takes his Christianity seriously I feel an immediate bond between us, whatever his race or education.

Under the lordship of Christ I am learning the significance of life and the secret of happiness: the assurance that amid the ups and downs of daily life there is always the steadfast love and care of almighty God. Success and failure alike are seen in the perspective of his infinite love. Now I look to the future not with anxiety but full of expectation, which gives wonder and spontaneity to life.

14
Christ helps me to live life to the full

I did all that my heart wanted to do, but I found it strangely unsatisfying after a time.

TALIB BARWANI was a nominal Muslim, for whom life had little meaning till he met Jesus through comrades in the Royal Air Force. Since writing this account, his ambition to serve Christ among Muslims has been fulfilled; he is on the staff of a Christian mission working in North Africa.

My forefathers were from Oman in Arabia; they settled in Zanzibar and inter-married with African people. My parents were very kind to me, and my mother in particular was a devout Muslim. I was sent to the Quran school, and learnt to read the Quran in Arabic (though I did not understand the meaning), to say my prayers five times a day, to fast in Ramadan and to give alms. When I was in my teens I had an urge to travel. After running away from home once or twice I succeeded in getting to Bombay. From there I went round the world as cabin boy on a cargo ship. I returned home, but after a year was off again, to India and the Persian Gulf. After working in various places I came to England to try to work and study, but my intentions were not realized and I began to live a dissolute life in London. I did all that my heart wanted to do, but I found it strangely unsatisfying after a time.

One day I was sitting in a café in the East End of London, feeling absolutely fed up with the sort of life I was living, when someone walked in with leaflets about joining the armed forces. I felt that any step would be in the right direction, so long as it took me away from the state I was in. So in 1957 I joined the Royal Air Force, and after drill and basic training in electronics I was posted to Libya. I enjoyed life in the R.A.F. and made many friends. I was friendly with a man from Norfolk called John, and we used to go swimming or walk around in Tobruk together.

One night I came back to the tent where we were living with four others and saw John on his knees, praying. This really took me aback, for I had never thought John was 'religious'. I admired his courage in being able to kneel down and pray in a tent full of people like us. As soon as he got up I asked him why he had suddenly become religious. He said it was not a question of being religious but of having Jesus Christ in his life. This was all strange to me, so he explained it. He told me how Jesus had come into the world to save sinners and had taken our place on the cross and borne the punishment which was justly ours; and how he now offers forgiveness and eternal life to anyone who will receive him into his heart and life by faith.

Though not a practising Muslim I still believed in Islam. I believed Jesus was a prophet like Abraham, Noah and Moses, but the idea that he was the Son of God was blasphemous to me. I pointed to certain countries which claimed to be Christian, yet ill-treated fellow human beings in the name of Christ. I contrasted this with the solid fellowship of Muslims from the Atlantic to China. What I did not know was that some Christians were praying earnestly for me.

One day at John's suggestion, though I was not really interested, I met Peter, another Christian, with an open Bible in his hands. He was a sergeant, and I noticed something different about him from other sergeants I knew. He showed me how Christ was predicted in the Old Testament and how in the New Testament he came to

70

fulfil those prophecies about himself. Then he turned to Revelation and read these words of the Lord Jesus, 'Behold, I stand at the door and knock; if any one hears my voice and opens the door, I will come in to him and eat with him, and he with me' (Revelation 3:20). These words went straight through to my heart. In spite of all that I had believed about Christians corrupting the New Testament, I knew these words were true. I knew that Jesus Christ was standing outside the door of my heart, knocking, and I was the only one who could open it or keep it closed. I did not want to make a decision, so I just took leave of Peter and went away.

I remember I went straight to the cinema to try and forget the experience, but the words of Jesus kept coming back to my mind, 'Behold, I stand at the door and knock . . .'. I kept telling myself this was silly and it was just a mood that would pass. I came out of the cinema intending to go to the NAAFI club and get drunk. Instead I went into a Nissen hut that was being used as a church and in there I completely broke down. I got down on my knees and prayed something like this, 'Lord Jesus, I know that you died on the cross for my sins. You are the Saviour from sin; please come into my life now as I open the door of my heart, and be my Saviour and Lord.' When I got up from my knees I had a deep peace and great joy. I knew that my sins were forgiven and I wanted to tell everyone about the wonderful experience I had just been through.

A month after my conversion I had an opportunity of going home to Zanzibar on holiday after about five years' absence from my people. I was afraid of what was going to happen when my people learnt that I was a Christian. People readily identify Christianity with Western imperialism. I tried to hide that I was a Christian when I saw how happy my mother and family were to see me. But within an hour of my arrival a situation developed in which I had to declare my new faith in Christ or deny him. My family could not understand why I had 'done this to them'. They were very distressed, and so was I because I loved my

71

mother. I cannot expect anyone who is not a true Christian to understand that my love for the Lord Jesus Christ must come before my love for the dearest members of my family, however much I loved them. In short, there were tears, misunderstandings and distress of heart on both sides.

Since that time God has been very real to me. I have had opportunities of proving his nearness when the going was tough. Jesus satisfies the deepest longings of my heart, and I have never regretted even for a moment the decision I made nearly ten years ago to open the door of my heart to him. The Lord has given me a wonderful wife from Lebanon who shares my faith, and we have two children for whom we thank God. We have been wanting to serve the Lord in Muslim lands, but so far all doors have been closed. While working in an electronics firm, however, I found increasing opportunities of preaching and giving my testimony in various churches round about Chelmsford.

My faith in Christ helps me to live life to the full. Whereas before life was at times boring or full of worries or just meaningless, today I am really happy that life has meaning, and the Lord has taught me not to worry about any situation that may confront me. Instead I have learnt to bring everything, big or small, to him in prayer and leave it with him. He has taught me not to hate anyone, no matter what they have done or said to me. I have a great sense of security that does not come by what I possess but by trusting God completely.

The Christian life is not easy, but it is the most wonderful, exciting and soul-satisfying life that I have ever known. This is why, whenever my wife and I have an opportunity, there is nothing that we enjoy more than telling to others the good news of God's great love for men in Jesus Christ.

15
It was all that I had longed for

I want to say that I received God's power and the grace of salvation not because I understood anything about it, but because his power was so great.

MARYAM, a young Indonesian, began to read the Bible almost by accident. She was drawn to Christ both by this and by the fellowship of the Christians with whom she began to associate. At length she took the decisive step and found a new peace and contentment. So she seeks to live 'in the love of Jesus Christ' and has a deep concern for those who do not yet know that love.

Normally someone is attracted to follow a particular faith or way of life when he knows something about its background, even though his knowledge is inadequate. But my experience was very different. I would feel ashamed if I had to tell of the evil that was in my heart. But as I write this it serves as a mirror of my own life, and I want to say that I received God's power and the grace of salvation not because I understood anything about it, but because his power was so great.

I was born a Muslim and did my best to meet the requirements of Islam. This was natural for me since all my ancestors were followers of the Islamic faith, which required them to train their descendants in the way of life which they themselves followed. You may ask if I knew Islam well and had any assurance that my religion would bring me salvation for eternity. The answer is 'No'.

I saw that Islamic teachings were good; indeed in many ways they are not so different from what was taught by Jesus Christ. For example, in Islam we find good instructions on how to behave and what to do in certain situations, as in the Sermon on the Mount. But one thing I was uncertain about was what would be the result of all that I did as a Muslim. The other question that was always occurring to me was whether I was just doing what I was told to do because I had been taught so since I was little. In practice I had to admit that this was indeed the case. Further, it did not seem to me that anyone really cared whether I believed or not. Perhaps I am not the only Indonesian who has had this experience, for most people in this country merely carry out the obligations as I did – because it was the faith they received from their parents.

I would like to tell you how I was attracted to the Christian religion, though it is impossible to tell exactly how it happened. I always wonder why this should have happened to me, but it was obviously God's leading so that I might be saved. The process by which I came to believe was very simple. A man carrying a Bible came to visit my brother, and while they were talking I looked into it. I enjoyed reading it and could understand some of it. But before I had read very much he left, taking the Bible with him. Because I had been so attracted to it and had enjoyed reading it so much, I borrowed a Bible from a Christian minister. He was surprised because he knew I was not a Christian.

After reading the Bible over and over again, I had a great desire to know more about the secrets it contained. I was especially impressed by the books of Genesis and St Matthew, and I felt a strong urge to act on what I read. But I was still not brave enough to tell anyone about it, so I kept silent. I had no friend whom I could ask for help or whom I could question about the life of Christians. I was too bashful to go to church, because I did not yet know what people did when they went to a church, even though my heart was always urging me to go.

At length in December 1967 I confessed the Christian faith and began to attend the Christian Religion classes at school, though I had never gone to church and knew nothing at all about what Christians did. In 1968 I moved to a boarding school. All the other students in my hostel were Christians, so when they went to church I went along with them. This was the starting-point of my dedication; I made a resolution to enter the fellowship of believers. I became active in church and began to be bolder and to be open and frank with my parents.

There were still many obstacles to be overcome, for after it became known that I had become a member of the Christian family, my parents and other relatives decided not to give me their permission to be baptized, though they did not say anything about my going to church and being active there. At that time I did not want to offend them, and I realized that baptism is not the ground of our salvation in Jesus Christ. I continued to take an active part in the church, and now I had many Christian friends. I carried on living in this way for four years. As I came to know more about Christian fellowship, I found it very attractive; it was all that I had longed for before I ever became a Christian.

Then on December 24th 1972, with all my heart and soul and with great determination, I asked to be officially received into the fellowship and so was baptized, despite the fact that I was going through a period of severe persecution. On entering fully into the fellowship I began to long after the sort of life which other believers were experiencing. Now I felt happier, more at peace, more content and steadfast, and began to understand why it was I believed in this faith and had entered the Christian life. There is probably no one main reason that can be given to explain why I feel my relationship with God to be closer now than ever before, but I am now more at peace and surrendered more fully to God's plan.

Am I proud of myself for having the hope that I have been accepted as a person fit to stand before God? Am I proud because I understand now that I am a sinner? No, of course not. But I very much desire to live as other persons have lived in the love of Jesus Christ, because what I have felt as a Christian is very different from what I experienced in the past. I feel the greatness of God's love. God has answered my prayers. This is a revelation which has come to me after living in the love of Jesus Christ.

It is my great concern to help those who have not yet heard the good news of God's salvation. I feel that we cannot afford not to be concerned for those around us who do not yet know the Saviour nor have yet received salvation based on Christ's love. There are so many who think that they know God, but really they only know about him. They have not yet received his salvation. Their hearts have not yet been opened to receive the news of salvation through Christ, and this is a very serious matter. Many people think their good deeds are sufficient to please God but do not yet understand the real meaning of what they have done or whether they will one day enter the kingdom of heaven. We must seek to bring such people really to know God through Christ.

A brief statement
of the Christian faith

There is one true and living God, himself Spirit, Creator of all spirits, human and angelic, and of all the vast universe which science has disclosed to us. He alone is eternal and self-existent; all else depends for its existence on him. He is present throughout his universe in every place and every age, but he makes himself known in particular places and times. The record of this self-disclosure of God is found supremely in the Scriptures of the Old and New Testaments (The Torah, Zabur and Injil). Actual copies exist today of Old Testament books in the original Hebrew, from before the Christian era, and of New Testament books in the original Greek from before AD 300 (*i.e.* several centuries before the Prophet Muhammad), and translations of the Bible are based on these. There are many minor variations between different ancient copies (manuscripts *etc.*), but none of these is important. There is not the slightest evidence of Jews or Christians deliberately altering these Scriptures or of any different Torah or Injil existing at or before the time when the Prophet said, 'God revealed the Torah and the Injil' (Quran 3:3).

That God is one is a basic tenet of the Torah of Moses. It is repeated several times in the Injil and has always been the faith of Christians. At the same time, the experience of the early disciples as they observed the life of Jesus and listened to his words, brought them to the conviction (supported by his own claims) that he was in a unique sense divine – 'My Lord and my God' in the words of one of them. Further when the Holy Spirit of God descended on the waiting disciples after Jesus' ascension and according to his clear promise, they came to see that God was working unseen among men, not just as a power or influence but personally. Hence the Holy Spirit too was held to be personal. Traditionally Christians have spoken of three 'Persons' in the one God – the Holy Trinity; but 'Person' here must not be taken in its ordinary meaning. The divine 'Persons' are linked in the unity of the Godhead more closely than human persons could ever be with each other. No earthly analogies can do justice to the divine Trinity; is it any wonder that human minds cannot fully grasp the mystery of our wonderful God, who is in a true sense *Al Ghaib* ('the Hidden One')? We can no more comprehend his greatness and his mystery than (to use a homely illustration) my cat can follow what I am doing when I read a book or pray. But no explanation of the Trinity is acceptable which does not affirm the unity of God.

Through the ages God sent his prophets to reveal to people his will and something of his nature and to call them to repentance and obedience. But when the right moment came, God himself took the form of a human being in the person of Jesus, Son of Mary, not so as to blot out his deity, so that he should merely *seem* to be a man, but so that the divine and human natures were marvellously combined in one person. In calling him 'Son of God', there is no reference to his miraculous conception, for he is that from all eternity, and it would be blasphemous to think of the glorious God somehow assuming a body and having physical relations with a human being (Mary), however holy. The term is a metaphor which speaks of one who possesses his Father's nature (as human sons do) and is nearest to the Father's heart. As man he was hungry, thirsty and tired; he sorrowed, was tempted, suffered and died; and at the same time, through his life of perfection, disclosed what God meant human life to be like. As God he revealed the divine glory through his whole life and triumphed over death in his resurrection. By his suffering for mankind, by offering himself as a perfect sacrifice for human sin, he disclosed the amazing love of God, for love in its very nature entails suffering, and a loving God must therefore be a suffering God – that is why the symbol of the cross means so much to Christians. His disciple could say, 'The Son of God loved me and gave himself for me', and this sacrificial love has supplied a tremendous motive for love and service in those who follow him.

Why did he have to suffer? Because, since Adam, men and women have been sinners, rebels against the holy God and deserving of God's judgement. No amount of good works or self-imposed sufferings could compensate for the sins even of a good person. Only the sacrifice of the perfect Man, who was himself God, could suffice to set people free and to blot out their sins. By taking away sins Christ's sacrifice re-establishes the link between God and mankind, so that people can receive God's gifts of free forgiveness and new life, eternal life, in the fellowship of the risen Christ. By faith alone mankind can receive God's amazing mercy offered in Christ; but this faith is not merely believing with the mind – it includes trusting Christ with the heart and committing one's will to him. Thus there is no question of Christ's atonement setting individuals free to go and sin again, as some have said; they are new people and no longer desire to do so.

New life in Christ involves the gift of the Holy Spirit, who enters our lives and gradually produces in us the qualities of Jesus Christ: love, joy, peace, patience, kindness, goodness, faithfulness, gentleness and self-control. But this involves our active co-operation and our use of the means God has given us for spiritual growth: worship together with other Christians, personal prayer and the intelligent study of, and meditation on, the Bible, not the mere repetition of its words. The Holy Spirit strengthens us for Christ's service and gives us special gifts which can be used to help others and to build up the Christian fellowship.

Finally, one day, as Jesus promised, God will intervene

again in human history through the return of Jesus Christ in glory, putting an end to the present age, so that the world we now know will vanish away. The Christian looks forward, then or after his own death, to life in the immediate presence of God unhindered by the presence and power of sin, in that heavenly kingdom where all wrongs will be righted and God's people will enjoy for ever the perfect vision of his beauty.